The Concise Illustrated Book of
Trees

Philip Perry

Brian Trodd Publishing House Limited

Published in 1990 by
Brian Trodd Publishing House Limited
27 Swinton Street, London WC1X 9NW

ISBN 1 85361 140 9

Printed in Portugal

Acknowledgments
A–Z Botanical Collection Ltd: 9, 15,
19, 20, 21, 22, 23, 42, 45, 46.
Ardea London Ltd: 13, 29, 32, 34, 35;
John Clegg 24; Bob Gibbons 31, 36; A.
Greensmith 40; A. P. Paterson 44; John
E. Swedberg 38; Wardene Weisser 18.
Harry Smith Horticultural Collection: 16,
25, 33, 37, 39; Polunin Collection 7,
17.
NHPA: 11, 41.
Oxford Scientific Films Ltd: Caroline
Aitzetmuller 30; Demi Bown 43; Neil
Bromhall 26; Terry Heathcote 8, 12,
14; G. A. Maclean 28; Stan Osolinski
10; David Wright 27.

All artworks by David More/Linden Artists.

CONTENTS

INTRODUCTION

Flowering plants are divided into two groups, known as Classes, gymnosperms and angiosperms. The gymnosperms include conifers, yews and the ginkgo. The angiosperms are made up of all the other flowering plants and display a bewildering variety of forms – from the lady's slipper orchid and the foxglove, to the bramble and the mighty oak. All trees are flowering plants although some of the non-flowering cycads and tree-ferns do have a somewhat tree-like appearance. Trees, like shrubs, differ from other types of flowering plants by their development of woody tissues. Trees are perennials, that is they live for more than two years, and they usually flower every year, although some of the longer-lived species only begin producing flowers after ten or more years. However, they continue to live and flower for many hundreds of years. In general trees have one main stem or trunk at ground level, though higher up the trunk may divide. (By comparison shrubs have many stems that arise from the base.) They bear lateral branches and can reach immense dimensions of height and girth. There can be a considerable degree of overlap between small trees and large shrubs. A tree such as hawthorn can also be grown as a shrub. If it is constantly trimmed, as in a hedge, its habit will be shrub-like, but given enough space and freedom from pruning it will grow naturally into a tree.

Trees under pressure

Trees are a vital part of our environment which have come under increasing pressure from man's activities in recent decades. Huge areas of natural forests have been cut down to supply man's seemingly endless greed for timber and more agricultural land. At present an area of tropical rainforest the size of 40 soccer pitches is being cut down every minute of the day. Unchecked, tree felling removes the soil's greatest protector and in many parts of the world this has led to devastating floods and loss of valuable topsoil. Tropical forests are particularly rich in species diversity and continued logging could put some of the rarer species at risk of extinction before their full potential has even been evaluated. As many pharmaceutical products including quinine, used to treat malaria, come from such trees this is patently short sighted. Trees, like all green plants, produce the oxygen we need to breathe as a by-product of their metabolism. As a consequence they play an enormous role in the delicate balance of the global environment and must be conserved at all costs. The effect of their destruction on the world's climate is still poorly understood, but it is certainly tremendously important.

Trees are a renewable resource and must be treated as such. Replanting must always follow after logging. Forest clearing is not the only problem, though. In Britain over 160,000 km (100,000 miles) of hedgerows have been dug up, removing many valuable wildlife habitats. Unplanned forest fires lay waste enormous areas of forest each year. Acid rain has also claimed the lives of countless trees. Some years back Dutch Elm Disease was accidentally introduced to Britain on imported timber, resulting in the death of millions of elm trees. Fortunately there seems at last to be a growing international realization that this wholesale destruction cannot be allowed to continue unchecked. It is to be hoped that with fuller international cooperation, the future will be brighter.

Tree identification

This can seem a daunting task at first, but like any activity it becomes easier with practice. A good place to start is at a local botanical garden or arboretum. Here the trees will be clearly labelled allowing you to begin associating each tree's visual characteristics with its name. Gradually you will be able to recognize the 'jizz' of a species, that is to say the intangible traits which, taken together, form a design unique to each species. This book provides an introduction to a greater knowledge and understanding of trees and, through this, to an increased awareness of the natural world

Family: Pine, Pinaceae
Distribution: Native to Europe and introduced to Britain in 1603
Crown: Narrowly conic
Height: To 50 m (164 ft)
Foliage: The short, dark green needles spread either side of the shoot in thick layers

Bark: Smooth and silver-grey, hence the name. In old trees the bark cracks into small square plates

Flowers and cones: The small, yellow male flowers grow in clusters. The upright, green female flowers are found in the upper part of the tree. They develop into tall cylindrical orange-brown cones.

General remarks: In Europe it exists in vast natural monocultures such as the Black Forest in West Germany. In Britain it was grown extensively in large man-made forests for its light, quick-growing timber. Because it is an alien species (i.e. introduced), these plantations were almost devoid of wildlife as few native animals were adapted to such a habitat. Birds such as Hen Harriers used the young plantations as breeding sites, but being ground nesters they moved away once the trees formed a canopy. Since the trees are susceptible to attack by greenfly they have mostly been replaced by the Grand Fir as a forestry tree. The soft white wood is utilized for indoor woodwork or pulp. Other products include various types of turpentine. The common Silver Fir was originally used as the Christmas tree but has now been superceded by the Norway Spruce. Bank Voles often eat the vegetative buds and if this is continually repeated it can turn young trees into a bush.

Abies alba

DOUGLAS FIR

Family: Pine, Pinaceae
Distribution: Native to western North America from British Columbia to Mexico. Introduced to Britain in 1827
Crown: Narrowly conic
Height: Perhaps the tallest tree ever, a specimen felled in British Columbia in 1895 was an incredible 128 m (420 ft). Today, trees of 90 m (300 ft) exist in the U.S.A. In Britain they can reach 55 m (180 ft)
Foliage: The flattened, green needles are soft and spread each side of the shoot. The leaves give off a sweet scent when crushed
Bark: Smooth, grey-green and bearing resin blisters when young, turning dark purple. Old trunks are heavily fissured and frequently corky
Flowers and cones: The whitish male flowers grow towards the shoot tips. The yellowish female flowers form pendent, dull brown, ovoid cones, 8 cm (3 in) long.
General remarks: Growth is very rapid, particularly on the moist Pacific coast, up to 1.5 m (5 ft) per annum, but it needs good soil. It grows in vast natural forests, both pure stands and mixed with other conifers, which are extensively exploited for building-timber and plywood. Its timber production is greater than any other tree in the U.S.A. It is much used in reforestation in America where it is also a popular Christmas tree. The strong, dur-able wood is sometimes sold as Oregon or Columbian pine. It is widely planted in Britain for pit props, telegraph poles and for pulping. The foliage is browsed by elk and mule deer and the seeds eaten by mice and Red Crossbills.

Pseudotsuga menziesii

Family: Pine, Pinaceae
Distribution: Eastern U.S.A. north to astern Canada. Introduced to Britain in ne 18th century, it is grown as an ornamental

Crown: Usually conical but sometimes rather round-topped
Height: 18–23 m (59–75 ft)
Foliage: The flat, bright shiny green needles are arranged in two or three rows on either side of the shoot. Unusually there is also another row growing along the centre of the shoot. The leaves soon fade to a dark green and have two white bands underneath
Bark: Orange-brown when young, becoming dull purple-brown with many deep furrows and ridges
Flowers and cones: The male flowers, which are yellow-green, are borne on two- to three-year-old shoots. The female flowers produce small oval cones that turn brown as they ripen and contain long-winged seeds.
General remarks: Also known as Canadian Hemlock or Hemlock spruce, this species prefers acid soils in cool moist valleys up to 1,500 m (4,920 ft). Previously its timber had no commercial value, but as wood shortages become more severe it is being increasingly utilized for pulp. The bark was once an important source of tannin, the substance used to tan leather. Often seen in pure stands it is also grown as a hedge plant. Whitetail Deer and Snowshoe Hares browse its twigs and Red Squirrels and Ruffed Grouse feed themselves heartily on the seeds.

Tsuga canadensis

9

LODGEPOLE PINE

Family: Pine, Pinaceae

Distribution: Mexico and southern California to Alaska. It has been in Britain since 1854. In more recent years it has been widely planted for timber in Britain and Europe

Crown: Open domed

Height: 6–25 m (20–80 ft)

Foliage: The long, twisted needles are borne in pairs and are yellow-green or deep green in colour. The buds exude resin

Bark: Light brown or dark red-brown, finely scaled

Flowers and cones: The male flowers are orange-brown. The red female flowers give rise to small conical cones bearing scales with spiny tips. The cones remain closed on the tree for years, often only opening after exposure to a forest fire which enables the species to quickly reseed burnt areas.

General remarks: The name refers to the use of the slender, straight trunks by North American Indians to support their tepees and lodges. A different variety of this species, the Beach or Shore Pine, is found in the coastal belt whereas the Lodgepole or Tamarack, as it is also known, is found further inland in the Rocky Mountains. The timber is similar to that of Scots Pine and is used for like purposes. Forests of th tree are the favoured habitat of the Lodg pole Chipmunk and the Spruce Grouse.

Pinus contorta

Family: Pine, Pinaceae

Distribution: Eastern North America. It was brought to England in 1743 but is still a rarity

Crown: Broadly domed

Height: 15–20 m (50–66 ft)

Foliage: The yellow-green needles grow in clusters of three, occasionally two or five. They are very long, stiff, quite thick and are often twisted

Bark: Yellowish brown, cracked into deep furrows and scaly plates

Flowers and cones: The small, purple male flowers are oval. The bright red female flowers turn into small, cylindrical, red-brown cones. The cones, which have stout, sharp thorns, frequently remain on the tree for many years.

General remarks: This is one of only two American species of pine that produce tufts of leafy shoots directly on the trunk, particularly after fires, to which it shows great resistance. It grows on poor sandy or rocky soils on steep slopes and in river valleys. The rather knotty wood is very resinous. Once used as a principal source of resin, the tree is now most important for its pulp and timber. The early colonials used it to make the pitch and tar needed to preserve their wooden ships.

Pinus rigida

NORWAY SPRUCE

Family: Pine, Pinaceae
Distribution: Native to continental Europe it is now naturalized in Britain. It is widely grown in North America for ornament and forestry
Crown: Pyramidal
Height: To 60 m (200 ft) on the continent, to 45 m (150 ft) in Britain
Foliage: The soft, dark green needles, on either side of the shoot, are short and upward pointing. When the needles are shed they leave a small peg-like projection which gives the twig a rough feel
Bark: Thin, smooth and red-brown
Flowers and cones: The small, round, reddish male flowers are found at the end of shoots. The red female flowers produce long, cylindrical, green cones that hang down and ripen brown.
General remarks: Initially a fast grower, it slows down after reaching 20 m (66 ft). It has replaced the Common Silver Fir as the Christmas tree. Although one of the world's most important timber trees, in Britain its relative the Sitka Spruce is now preferred by foresters. The light strong wood, often marketed as white deal, is used in interior woodwork as it is not durable outdoors unless treated with preservatives. In the building trade it is used for rafters, flooring and joists. Its resonant quality makes it admirably suited for making violins and cellos. It is the premier wood for producing paper pulp, particularly for newspapers, and most timber is put to this use. Red Deer eat the shoots and bark, and Red Squirrels enjoy the male flower buds which they scoop out with their incisors. Crossbills have specially adapted bills which enable them to remove the seeds from the cones.

Picea abies

Family: Pine, Pinaceae
Distribution: Native to Scotland and most of Europe across to eastern Siberia. It naturalized in England where it has been grown since the 1600s. It is widely planted in the U.S.A. and south-eastern Canada
Crown: Flat-topped or rounded, high on long bare bole (trunk)

Height: Up to 35 m (115 ft)
Foliage: The relatively short, thick, blue-green leaves grow in pairs and are frequently twisted
Bark: Orange-brown, flaking in upper crown and deeply fissured into broad flat plates on the lower trunk
Flowers and cones: The yellow male flowers are found at the base of shoots. The globular, crimson female flowers generate bright green conical cones. These mature the following year into short-stalked, grey-brown, pendent cones.
General remarks: It flourishes on poor, dry soils such as sandy heaths. The soft wood is extremely good for general construction work including rafters, flooring, joists and pit-props as well as being pulped. Treated with creosote it is used outside for telegraph poles and railway sleepers. The resin is used to produce turpentine, rosin, tar and pitch. In North America it is mostly grown for ornament. The Caledonian Scots Pine forests, where mature trees can be 250 years old, are incredibly rich wildlife habitats. Red Squirrels and Roe Deer abound together with Crested Tits, Scottish Crossbills and Ospreys while the forest floor is carpeted with a mass of bilberries and juniper. Three-toed Woodpeckers often leave chisel-shaped marks on the bark in their quest for insects. Capercaillies eat the fresh shoots and needles.

Pinus sylvestris

WESTERN HEMLOCK

Family: Pine, Pinaceae
Distribution: Western North America from northern California to Alaska. Introduced to Britain in 1851
Crown: Conical but broader in older trees. The leading shoot droops
Height: In the U. S. A. it reaches 70 m (230 ft) while in Britain it has grown to 50 m (164 ft)
Foliage: The short, flat needles vary in size on each shoot. They are bright green, darkening with age
Bark: Smooth, dark grey-green turning dark brown, it flakes and shreds
Flowers and cones: The small, red male flowers are dense on even the lowest shoots on old trees. The plum-coloured female flowers produce small pale brown, pendulous, egg-shaped cones in great quantities on small branchlets.
General remarks: The largest hemlock, it grows quickly and can increase by 1 m (3½ ft) in a year. Found up to 1,800 m (5,900 ft) it tolerates shade well when young but cannot grow in polluted air. The name derives from the aromatic smell of its leaves which resembles that of the European herb, Hemlock. The pale brown timber is used mainly for paper pulp, but also in building and for producing cellulose. The bark is still utilized for tanning leather and once was made into a coarse bread by the Alaskan Indians. It is grown commercially in Britain in increasing quantities.

Tsuga heterophylla

Family: Pine, Pinaceae
Distribution: Northern U.S.A., Canada

and Alaska. It was brought to Britain by 1700 but is still uncommon
Crown: Narrowly conic
Height: 12–30 m (40–100 ft)
Foliage: The short, pale blue-green needles stand erect on the shoots and are sharply pointed. The leaves have a faint mousy or skunk-like smell when bruised
Bark: Greyish, with large round plates when old
Flowers and cones: The small, cylindrical, orange-brown cones have thin woody scales and drop as soon as they mature.
General remarks: One of North America's most widely distributed trees, it is sometimes referred to as Canadian or Skunk Spruce. It favours waterside habitats and may grow in pure stands. In exposed mountainous situations the tree has a mat-like habit. It is grown for timber infrequently in northern Europe. In Canada, however, it is the most important commercial species. It is the premier pulpwood and also provides construction timber. It is used for the sounding boards of pianos and other musical instruments. The seeds are a staple food of the Sitka Mouse. The northern spruce forests are the customary haunt of White-winged and Red Crossbills, Pine and Evening Grosbeaks, American Three-toed Woodpeckers and the Spruce Grouse.

Picea glauca

WESTERN RED CEDAR

Thuja plicata

Family: Cypress, Cupressaceae
Distribution: California north to Alaska. Introduced to Britain in 1854
Crown: Narrowly conic
Height: 30–50 m (100–164 ft)
Foliage: The aromatic flattened scale leaves, reminiscent of fern fronds, which are characteristic of cypresses, are bright yellowish green
Bark: Fibrous, dark purple-brown, ridged with large vertical plates stripping off
Flowers and cones: The tiny, pale yellow male flowers are borne on the shoot tips. The similarly small female flowers produce small brown cones consisting of only a few scales.
General remarks: They grow nearly 1 m ($3\frac{1}{2}$ ft) each year until they reach 30 m (100 ft), but then development slows considerably. The Indians of western North America chose to carve their totem poles from the wood of this tree. War canoes were hollowed from giant trunks, giving it the name of Canoe Cedar. They are planted in Britain and Europe for the straight-grained, light but durable timber. Although particularly resistant against rot in North America, in Britain the wood must be treated with preservative if it is to be used outside as the climate is not suitable for natural seasoning. It is used for making fencing, telegraph poles, ladders and sheds as well as roofing shingles. It makes a good hedge or windbreak and the distinctive foliage is popular with florists for flower arrangements and wreaths.

Family: Yew, Taxaceae
Distribution: Native to Britain, it is also found in Europe, North Africa and east to the western Himalayas. It is widely grown in North America as an ornamental
Crown: Very broad or pyramidal-shaped
Height: An evergreen tree or shrub growing to 20 m (66 ft)
Foliage: The short dark green leaves, borne in two rows, are narrow and linear.

Poisonous to man and cattle they can be eaten harmlessly by deer and rabbits. The leaves often form galls caused by the Yew-gall Midge
Bark: Red-brown, thin, breaks away in long flakes
Flowers and fruit: Trees are either male or female (dioecious). The yellowish green male flowers are rather insignificant. Female trees bear small, bright red, fleshy fruits known as arils. The greenish black seeds are eaten by Hawfinches and Nut-hatches but are poisonous to many mammals. Though yews are wind-pollinated, the male flowers are visited by bees which collect the pollen.
General remarks: The longevity of Yew is well known, though often exaggerated; nevertheless a few are probably more than 1,000 years old. Although old trees often become hollow they continue growing as well as ever, but their age is then very difficult to calculate accurately as their annual rings cannot be counted. Yew favours chalk and limestone soils. The dark red wood is famous for its ancient use in making English longbows, its slow growth producing the ideal qualities of strength and elasticity demanded for this purpose. It is a superior wood for cabinet making. Yews can be clipped for hedging and to create the finest examples of topiary in the world.

Taxus baccata

ASPEN

Populus tremula

Family: Willow, Salicaceae

Distribution: Native to Britain and Europe extending as far north as the Arctic circle

Crown: Open

Height: 25 m (80 ft)

Foliage: The dark green, rather rounded leaves are deeply and bluntly toothed with a wavy margin. Initially they are tinged with a copper colour and in autumn they turn yellow. They vary greatly in size on different parts of the tree, from 1–10 cm ($\frac{1}{2}$–4 in). As they have very narrow leaf-stalks they quiver in the slightest breeze. The buds are slightly sticky

Bark: Greenish grey, smooth with conspicuous horizontal lenticels (raised pores)

Flowers and fruit: Aspens, like all poplars, are either male or female (dioecious). The grey-brown male catkins are pendulous and covered with long silky white hairs. The green female catkins are also silky-haired, though to a much lesser extent than the male flowers. They bear white woolly seeds, which are carried long distances by the wind.

General remarks: In Britain the Aspen is commonest in Scotland, notably on poor stony or sandy soils. It can withstand polluted air reasonably well and reproduces readily by root suckers. The light, soft, porous wood is sometimes used by sculptors and carvers. As the wood splits easily and burns slowly it has been used to make matchsticks. It also makes a good quality paper pulp. European Beavers are very fond of gnawing the bark, shoots and leaves of this tree.

Family: Willow, Salicaceae

Distribution: Native to Britain, it occurs in Europe west to Siberia. It was introduced in colonial times to North America and is now established in parts of eastern U.S.A. and eastern Canada

Crown: Broadly conic. Old trees may be heavily twisted

Height: Grows to 25 m (80 ft)

Foliage: The rich glossy green, glabrous leaves are narrowly lance-shaped (lanceolate) and 12 cm (5 in) long with finely toothed margins. The buds are sticky.

Bark: Grey-green, scaly when young becoming ridged and nearly black as it matures

Flowers and fruit: The male and female flowers are produced on separate trees. The male flowers form slender yellow catkins. The 10 cm (4 in) green female catkins develop thin, fluffy white seeds.

General remarks: This willow, which usually grows along rivers, is often pollarded. The name refers to the one-year-old branches which easily and loudly snap off at their base. These twigs, which can grow roots, often fall into a river and are carried downstream where they may lodge in mud and eventually produce a new tree. It often hybridizes with the White Willow. It is similar in appearance to the American Black Willow.

Salix fragilis

19

WEEPING WILLOW

Family: Willow, Salicaceae

Distribution: It is a familiar ornamental tree in Britain. The Chinese species, which has brown twigs, has been widely planted in North America, where it has become naturalized

Crown: Irregular, extremely broad-domed

Height: Up to 22 m (70 ft)

Foliage: The yellow shoots bear long leaves, a bright pale green above and whitish below. The leaves, narrowly lanceolate in shape, are glossy with fine hairs on both their upper and lower surfaces and have finely serrated margins

Bark: Pale grey-brown, roughened with ridges

Flowers and fruit: Male trees have flowers in the form of long upward curving yellow catkins borne at the ends of shoots. Unusually for a willow, female flowers are sometimes borne on the same tree as the male flowers.

General remarks: This tree exists in a number of different varieties and is known by several Latin names, a situation further complicated by the natural ease with which willows can hybridize. In Britain the commonest form is a hybrid resulting from a cross between the White Willow (*Salix alba*) and the Chinese or Golden Weeping Willow (*S. babylonica*). It is most commonly found alongside rivers and lakes especially in parks and large gardens. A fast growing tree, it is easily propagated from long twigs pushed deep into the soil

Salix × chrysocoma

Family: Willow, Salicaceae
Distribution: California north to Alaska. Introduced to Britain at the end of the 19th century

Crown: Initially conic but later quite broad-topped

Height: Generally 18–40 m (60–130 ft) it can reach 60 m (200 ft) in the U.S.A. but so far has only reached 35 m (115 ft) in Britain where it has been grown for less than 100 years

Foliage: The thick, yellowish green leaves have long tapering points and are oval with rounded serrations at the edge. The resinous buds and new foliage have a strong fragrance of balsam, giving rise to the name of this group of poplars

Bark: Dark green or black and smooth, becoming shallowly fissured when old

Flowers and fruit: Dioecious, the large hanging male catkins are dull red and develop before the new leaves sprout. Female flowers are green and produce three-valved capsules containing small seeds covered with white cotton-wool.

General remarks: Alternatively named Black Cottonwood or California Poplar it is the largest broadleaved tree in the Rocky Mountains of western America. The fastest growing tree in Britain, it can reach 30 m (100 ft) in only 15 years. Often found with alders and willows, it prefers moist soils in river valleys and flood plains. The wood is principally used for paper pulp, crates and veneers.

Populus trichocarpa

BLACK WALNUT

Juglans nigra

Family: Walnut, Juglandaceae

Distribution: Native to eastern U.S.A., it was brought to Britain before the 1650s, but it has never become commonplace. It is grown quite extensively in Central Europe for timber

Crown: High domed, rounded

Height: 20–30 m (66–100 ft)

Foliage: The dark green pinnate leaves have seven to twenty-three leaflets which are covered with soft hairs beneath. Unlike the common walnut the edges of each leaflet are serrated

Bark: Grey-black, deeply fissured

Flowers and fruit: The lime green, drooping male catkins can be 10 cm (4 in) long. The green female flowers are found in small clusters of three or five. The green fruit develops into a round, hard brown corrugated nutshell that contains the rather small, oily seed. The fruits usually occur in pairs and the nut is darker and rather less palatable than that of the common species.

General remarks: Mainly found on damp but well-drained soils, it is one of the U.S.A.'s rarest and most sought after native hardwoods. The dark brown, richly grained wood is a favourite for furniture and veneers, particularly as it takes polish well. It is also used for gunstocks owing to its unique ability to absorb the recoil. In America the sweet nuts are consumed by humans as well as squirrels and mice, and the husks can be utilized to make a yellow-brown dye. The tree is capable of poisoning nearby fruit trees with a poison in its roots.

Family: Walnut, Juglandaceae
Distribution: Most likely introduced by the Romans, it has become naturalized in Britain. It probably originated in central Asia, but since early times has been widely cultivated. It occurs naturally in south-east Europe across to China and has also been introduced to the U.S.A. where it is called the English Walnut
Crown: Spreading
Height: 30 m (100 ft)
Foliage: The dark green pinnate leaves have from three to nine ovate leaflets, which are very scented when crushed
Bark: Pale grey, smooth becoming furrowed with age
Flowers and fruit: The short, pendulous male catkins are dull brown and the erect green female flowers are formed at the end of shoots. The smooth green fruits mature through the summer until the outer fleshy layer decays to reveal the familiar wrinkled brown nutshell.
General remarks: The Common Walnut prefers deep, fertile chalk or limestone soils. The timber is very high grade and consequently much in demand. Its dark colour makes it a favourite of furniture and cabinet makers. It is also commonly used for rifle stocks. The large nuts are very nutritious and are produced commercially as a fresh food or for pickling. The nuts are borne after the tree's tenth year but they do require a good summer to ripen properly. In the U.S.A. it is planted for ornament as well as for its nuts. Walnuts are favoured in particular by Wood Mice and Jackdaws.

Juglans regia

COMMON ALDER

Alnus glutinosa

Family: Birch, Betulaceae

Distribution: Native to Britain and found in Europe across to Siberia and also in North Africa. It has been introduced to the northern United States and eastern Canada, where it is called the European Black Alder

Crown: Broadly conic, frequently on two or three trunks

Height: 25 m (80 ft)

Foliage: The large very dark green leaves are roughly oval with a wavy margin that is bluntly and shallowly toothed

Bark: Initially purplish becoming grey-brown, broken into small plates

Flowers and fruit: The male and female catkins, produced in late summer, do not open until the following spring. The pendulous male catkins are purplish until the yellow anthers become visible. The small, red, upright female flowers open before the leaves. The winged seeds, which develop in a blackish woody structure reminiscent of a tiny pine cone, are buoyant and are successfully distributed by rivers.

General remarks: The Common Alder favours riverside or marshy habitats to which it is adapted by virtue of the nitrogen-fixing bacteria in its root nodules. Frequently coppiced it sometimes occurs in woods called carrs. The soft yellowish wood can be made into barrels and small items such as matches as well as good quality charcoal. As it can withstand being immersed in water for long periods of time it has been also used for pilings. Different coloured dyes can be extracted from the tree. The seeds, when available, are a staple food of Redpolls and Siskins. The branches and bark are a favourite food of European Beavers, and Roe Deer sometimes fray the bark to mark their territory.

amily: Birch, Betulaceae
istribution: Northern U.S.A. and

Canada. Although introduced to Britain in 1750, it is uncommon, occasionally being planted as an ornamental specimen tree in gardens

Crown: Irregular

Height: To 20 m (66 ft)

Foliage: The oval dark green leaves vary in size from 4–10 cm (up to 4 in) and have a pointed tip. The buds are not covered in resin which helps distinguish this species from the similar silver birch

Bark: Initially bronze it becomes pure white but marked with long narrow lines. These curl up at the end and tear off in horizontal papery strips

Flowers and fruit: The pendulous male catkins are large. The smaller more slender female catkins also hang down and produce tiny fruit.

General remarks: The alternative name of Canoe Birch derives from the use of its bark by Indians to cover the cedar frames of their canoes. They also used it as a tepee covering, to make shoes and for other diverse purposes. Another name for this most beautiful tree is American White Birch. Preferring damp uplands it is one of the first trees to re-seed a burnt area. The timber is used as fuel and for pulp as well as small items such as ice-cream sticks and children's toys. The seeds are well liked by Sharp-tailed and Ruffed Grouse. Moose and deer often browse on the twigs.

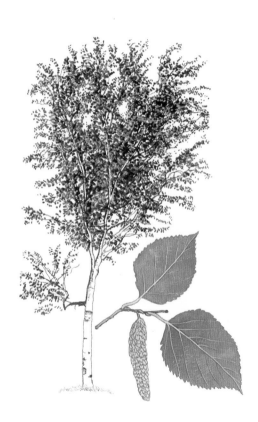

Betula papyrifera

25

SILVER BIRCH

Family: Birch, Betulaceae

Distribution: Native to Britain, it is also found throughout Europe as far north as the Arctic circle and east to Siberia. It has been introduced to North America as an ornamental

Crown: Young trees are narrowly conic, becoming domed with age

Height: To 30 m (100 ft)

Foliage: The small, bright green leaves are ace-of-spades shaped. The buds are coated with a resinous substance

Bark: The white, papery bark, which peels in thin slivers, contrasts with the black rectangular bosses on the trunk

Flowers and fruit: The small clusters of pendulous male catkins are yellow when pollen-covered. The pale green female flowers stand upright at first, then droop. The tiny winged fruits are the favoured autumn food of Redpolls and Siskins.

General remarks: Growing on poor acid soils, it lives up to 200 years. It is a pioneer species and as such is the first to appear after land has been burnt or cleared. Although birches are Britain's third commonest trees they are not very important for timber. Nevertheless the wood is used extensively in Scandinavia, where it is the only native hardwood in the far north, for plywood, furniture and also skis. In North America the tree is called the European White Birch.

Betula pendula

Family: Hazel, Corylaceae
Distribution: Native to Britain and Europe across to Asia Minor
Crown: Broad and shrubby

Height: A large shrub or small tree up to 10 m (33 ft)
Foliage: The large dark green leaves are oval or rounded with a toothed margin
Bark: Coppery brown, shiny with strips curling away
Flowers and fruit: The yellowish male catkins hang down and the small brown female flowers produce clusters of one to four green nuts in papery bracts which ripen brown.
General remarks: Favouring chalk and limestone soils it is a lowland species found only up to 600 m (1,970 ft). The old English name of Filbert is derived from the fact that the nuts ripen about St. Philibert's Day, 20 August. The wood is soft but flexible and has found use as hurdles and fence stakes and is frequently coppiced for this purpose. Coppices provide a favourite haunt for Nightingales. Sika strip the bark and the nuts or cob-nuts are much sought after by Red Squirrels as well as Jays which wedge them into a crevice in a log in order to crack them open with hammer blows from their beak. Though difficult to gnaw open Wood Mice, Hazel Dormice and Bank Voles are among the many rodents that feast on the nuts which are harvested commercially by man, particularly for use in confectionery. Twigs still retaining the catkins are often used as an indoor decoration in spring.

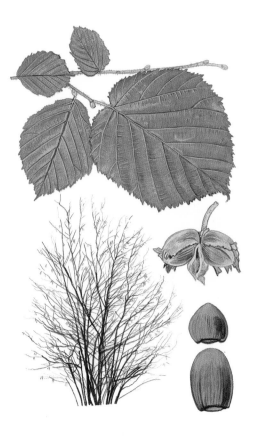

Corylus avellana

HORNBEAM

Family: Hazel, Corylaceae
Distribution: Native to southern England, it also occurs in Europe to Asia Minor. Very occasionally it is planted as an ornamental in the U.S.A.
Crown: Broadly conic
Height: To 25 m (80 ft)
Foliage: The short-stalked, narrowly oval, dark green leaves have a double-toothed margin and a wrinkled surface
Bark: Pale silver-grey with delicate brown stripes. In old trees the bark is deeply fluted
Flowers and fruit: The numerous, yellow-green male catkins hang down, as do the yellowish female catkins. The latter produce clusters of small green, three-lobed fruits, which ripen brown.
General remarks: Occurring mainly on heavy soils, it is common in Britain only in south-eastern England. Some varieties are found in town parks and streets and in a very few places it forms pure stands of woodland. In the past it was often coppiced or pollarded for firewood or good quality charcoal. Because the wood is very hard and tough it is difficult to work. These properties make it ideal for mallets and other wooden tools, as well as for piano hammers. It makes an excellent t[...] clipped hedge and is used in topiary. T[...] autumn colour of the foliage is good, if n[...] very spectacular. Its hard seeds are cracke[...] open by Greenfinches.

Carpinus betulus

SWEET GUM

Family: Witch-hazel, Hamamelidaceae
Distribution: Native to eastern and southern U.S.A. It has been introduced to Britain where it is now quite common
Crown: Domed

Height: To 35 m (115 ft) in the U.S.A. and to 28 m (90 ft) in Britain

Foliage: The five or seven lobed leaves are rather maple-like in appearance but, unlike maples, they are borne alternately not opposite. When crushed the leaves emit a resinous odour. The rich green, toothed leaves turn a brilliant scarlet, followed by yellow and purple, in the autumn

Bark: Grey or brown, becoming deeply fissured

Flowers and fruit: The small male flowers develop in erect spikes and the female flowers in dense yellow drooping clusters. The woody fruit consists of a burr-like group of capsules each of which contain two seeds, held at the end of a long stalk.

General remarks: The tree's name refers to the rather sweet sap that exudes from wounds. In North America this is used for preparing adhesives and other products. Often a pioneer species on newly logged areas, it is an important timber tree that is second only to the oaks for hardwood lumber production in America. Its red-brown wood, sometimes called Satin Walnut or Satinwood, polishes very well, hence its use for furniture, cabinet making and veneers. The seeds provide a nutritious food for numerous animals, including Chipmunks and Wild Turkeys.

Liquidambar styraciflua

HORSECHESTNUT

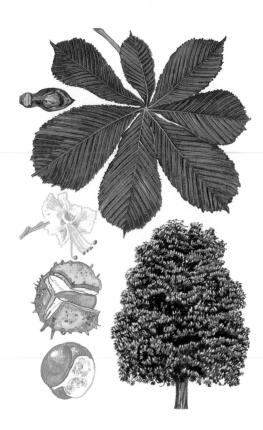

Aesculus hippocastanum

Family: Horsechestnut, Hippocastanaceae

Distribution: Although it originates from Asia and Eastern Europe, this common and very well-known tree has become naturalized in Britain where it has been grown for nearly 400 years. It is widely grown in continental Europe and North America as an ornamental shade and street tree

Crown: A massive tall, dense dome

Height: Up to 25 m (80 ft)

Foliage: The leaves are very big and consist of five to seven large leaflets that radiate from a point like spread fingers. The leaflets are bright green, becoming darker, and have serrated margins

Bark: Grey-brown or red-brown, becoming scaly and fissured

Flowers and fruit: The flowers are produced in upright panicles containing as many as 150 white-petalled flowers with a large yellow blotch at their base which turns red after a day or so. Up to three highly polished rich brown seeds or conkers are borne inside thickly fleshed, green rounded fruits covered with short, sharp spines.

General remarks: Extremely common in parks and large gardens, this magnificent tree creates plentiful shade. It is thought that the tree's name derives from the use of its seeds by Turks to prepare a remedy for curing horses' coughs. The favourite of every schoolboy, its seeds are much treasured for the traditional playground game of conkers. Its fine-grained timber is of little value though it can be used in cabinet making. Roe and Red Deer are among those wild animals that feast on the tree's abundantly produced conkers which are occasionally used as fodder for sheep and cattle.

Family: Beech, Fagaceae

Distribution: Native to southern England. It also occurs in western, central and southern Europe

Crown: Young trees conic, old trees massively domed

Height: To 40 m (130 ft)

Foliage: The leaf buds are long and sharply pointed. The shiny dark green, oval leaves have wavy margins and turn yellow then rich orange-brown in autumn

Bark: Smooth, metallic grey

Flowers and fruit: The male flowers are formed in yellowish drooping tassels at the end of a short stem. The enormous numbers of fallen flowers form a carpet under the tree. The female flowers grow in pairs and are small and held erect. The green fruit, produced in clusters of four, ripen to brown triangular nuts (beechmast) enclosed in a prickly husk. Beechmast is usually produced in greatest quantities in the season following a hot summer (a 'mast year').

General remarks: When grown as a hedge the Common Beech retains its bronze leaves all winter. Many ornamental varieties of beech exist such as those with copper or purple foliage, weeping branches and fastigiate or upright form ('Dawyck'). The fine-grained wood is relatively free from knots. It is used for furniture, parquet flooring and plywood. Beechmast has for centuries been used to feed livestock, particularly hogs. Nuthatches wedge the nuts in bark crevices either to crack them open or for a winter store. Bramblings, Badgers and Yellow-necked Mice forage for them on the ground. Red Squirrels sometimes strip the bark to eat the exposed growth layer. Short-tailed Voles sometimes gnaw the roots of saplings.

Fagus sylvatica

31

ENGLISH OAK

Quercus robur

Family: Beech, Fagaceae

Distribution: Native to lowland Britain, Europe, North Africa across to south-west Asia. It has been planted quite widely in northern U.S.A. and southern Canada, but is not common

Crown: Broad and spreading

Height: Up to 40 m (130 ft)

Foliage: The oblong, lobed leaves are dull dark green and are often attacked by insects, some of which cause the formation of galls known as oak-apples

Bark: Grey-brown, with rugged fissures in rectangular plates

Flowers and fruit: Both male and female catkins are greenish yellow, the former being the longer of the two. The green acorns sit in long-stalked cups, usually in pairs, and turn brown when ripe.

General remarks: Also called the Common or Pedunculate Oak, the latter name referring to the stalked (pedunculate) acorns. It is often pollarded and some such trees are estimated to be 600 years old. The dark brown, extremely heavy timber is demanded for the highest quality furniture, wall panelling and for barrels in which to mature sherry, whisky and cider. England's sailing ships of the past were constructed from it, as it is not only very strong but resistant to rotting. Up to 2,000 oak trees might be used to build one ship of the line but fortunately they could be long lived – Nelson's *Victory* served for years as an active warship and th remained afloat at moorings for a furth 87 years. These vigorous trees are partic larly valuable for the phenomenal varie of wildlife they support. A single healt tree has hundreds of millions of insects a other arthropods living on it, which turn provide food for many species birds and mammals.

RED OAK

Family: Beech, Fagaceae
Distribution: Native to eastern U.S.A. and eastern Canada. It has been introduced to Britain and Europe where it is grown for its wood
Crown: Conic when young, eventually broadly domed
Height: 18–35 m (60–115 ft)

Foliage: The dull dark green leaves vary somewhat in their shape but are generally oblong with moderately large, pointed lobes. They turn red, reddish brown or yellowish brown in autumn
Bark: Smooth, silver-grey with a few warts and relatively few fissures
Flowers and fruit: The drooping male catkins are yellowish. The tiny red female flowers develop into short-stalked acorns that take two years to mature.
General remarks: The Latin name *Quercus borealis* is used by some authorities for this species. It is sometimes called the Northern Red Oak in America to distinguish it from the Spanish or Southern Red Oak. Surprisingly for an oak it is very fast growing and can produce shoots of 2.5 m (about 8 ft) in a year. About half of the hardwood timber harvested in the U.S.A. each year is oak. The red-brown heartwood, which is not as good quality as that of the slower growing white oaks, is used for pilings, flooring, furniture and pulp. In America it is susceptible to a fungal disease necessitating fumigation of the timber before it can be exported to countries where the fungus does not yet occur. Many animals feed on the acorns including Bobwhite, Wild Turkey, Black Bear and Raccoon. Snowshoe Hares and Whitetail Deer browse on the foliage and Porcupines eat the inner bark.

Quercus rubra

LONDON PLANE

Family: Plane, Platanaceae

Distribution: This tree is a natural hybrid between the oriental plane and the American sycamore (also a species of plane tree), which first arose in France or Spain in the 17th century. It was soon introduced to Britain and in more recent years has been widely planted in North America

Crown: High domed

Height: Up to 50 m (164 ft) in Britain, to 20 m (66 ft) or so in the U.S.A.

Foliage: The large, glossy bright green leaves have five deeply cut lobes

Bark: The smooth, grey bark flakes off exposing the yellow inner bark

Flowers and fruit: The yellow male flowers and the reddish female flowers grow in spherical clusters. The fruits, small downy nuts, borne in globose heads, stay on the tree during winter, only falling off the following spring.

General remarks: It is the tallest broad-leaved tree in Britain and as specimens planted nearly 300 years ago are still robust it looks set to increase this record in the years to come. As it rarely sets fertile seed it is generally propagated from cuttings. It thrives in poor soils and even in a smoggy atmosphere. The hard, fine-grained wood is often known as lacewood and is used as a veneer in furniture making.

Platanus × hispanica

34

Family: Lime, Tiliaceae
Distribution: It is common throughout Britain and Europe. It has been introduced to the U.S.A. as an ornamental shade tree, particularly in the north

Crown: Tall domed
Height: At up to 40 m (130 ft) it is one of Britain's tallest broadleaved trees
Foliage: The broad ovate leaves are dull green with a pointed tip
Bark: Grey, smooth at first then finely ridged
Flowers and fruit: The tiny whitish flowers are fragrant, produced part way along a yellowish bract in hanging clusters of up to ten flowers. The hard fruits are roughly oval in shape but in Britain the seeds are rarely fertile.
General remarks: It is also sometimes called the European Lime, as suggested by its Latin name, and its old name of Linden is still used in North America. Unrelated to the Citrus-fruit Lime, it is a naturally occurring hybrid resulting from a cross between the large-leaved and small-leaved limes (*Tilia platyphyllos* and *T. cordata*) and its features are somewhat intermediate in character. The leaves are invariably attacked by vast numbers of aphids which produce a rain of sticky honeydew that falls onto anything beneath the tree and is quickly turned black by mould, making it totally unsuitable for roadside planting. It has soft, white wood which is used for carvings and in making musical instruments such as pianos. Bees produce a very fine, quite distinctively flavoured honey from its fragrant flowers.

Tilia × europaea

FIELD MAPLE

Family: Maple, Aceraceae
Distribution: Native to southern Britain, Europe, North Africa and western Asia. It has been introduced to the U.S.A., where it is called the Hedge Maple, but is rarely seen outside gardens
Crown: Low domed, occasionally high domed
Height: Up to 25 m (80 ft), usually less
Foliage: The leaves, which are pinkish at first then dark green, have five blunt lobes. Broken leaf-stalks exude a milky sap. Its leaves make a fine autumn display as they turn bronze, red and then yellow, particularly when grown as a hedge
Bark: Grey or pale brown with wide cracks and fissures
Flowers and fruit: The yellow-green male and female flowers grow together in one inflorescence (flower cluster). The fruits are reddish at first turning yellow and are borne in fours with horizontal wings
General remarks: Most common on chalky and limestone soils, especially in hedgerows, it is sometimes called the Common Maple. Although ideal in small gardens it is seldom planted nowadays. The white or brownish wood, which has a very fine grain, is quite rare but was used for turning or carving as well as by cabinet makers in the 19th century.

Acer campestre

Family: Maple, Aceraceae

Distribution: Native to east and central North America it has been planted in western regions. It was brought to Britain as long ago as 1656 but has never been widely grown

Crown: Tall, domed

Height: 18–30 m (60–100 ft)

Foliage: The three- to five-lobed leaves are reddish at first, becoming dark green, with hairy silver undersides and coarse teeth along the margins. The leaves produce a remarkable array of autumn colours, from scarlet through to gold. The twigs and buds are also reddish

Bark: Pale grey, smooth until older when it darkens and peels off in strips

Flowers and fruit: Groups of red, occasionally yellow, flowers emerge in short clusters before the tree regains its leaf cover. The bright reddish fruits, formed in winged pairs, ripen in late spring.

General remarks: A fast-growing tree, it particularly likes moist or swampy soils such as river banks. Also known as Swamp or Scarlet Maple, it is normally found in mixed hardwood forests. It is often grown as an ornamental shade tree. While not of major importance the lumber is sometimes used to make furniture.

The branches are browsed by Eastern Cottontails and Snowshoe Hares.

Acer rubrum

SUGAR MAPLE

Acer saccharum

Family: Maple, Aceraceae
Distribution: Eastern North America across to Texas. It was introduced to Britain in 1735
Crown: Open and irregular, dense
Height: 20–30 m (66–100 ft)
Foliage: The pale green leaves have five sharply-pointed lobes, with a few large teeth along the margins. This tree produces the most spectacular display of autumn colour of all the maples. Its leaves turn flame red, orange, gold and scarlet, making it a popular ornamental tree
Bark: Smooth, dark brown becoming deeply grooved and ridged with age, when large plates peel away
Flowers and fruit: Formed in clusters the flowers are yellowish. The winged green fruits occur in pairs and ripen brown in the autumn.
General remarks: It prefers moist upland soils. The sap is boiled to prepare the renowned maple syrup and sugar. A single tree can yield around 8 litres (2 gallons) of syrup or 4 kg (9 lb) of sugar. The leaf is the national symbol of Canada. In some areas the tree has fared badly in recent years, possibly due to acid rain. Much esteemed for furniture, the timber's other products include veneers and flooring. Some forms produce unusual grain patterns which are greatly coveted. Porcupines will eat the bark and Whitetail Deer browse the twigs.

Family: Maple, Aceraceae
Distribution: Originally from central and southern Europe, it was introduced to Britain by the Romans and so popularly regarded as a native species. It is grown in gardens in the U.S.A. and on occasions is found growing wild

Crown: Broadly domed

Height: To 35 m (115 ft)

Foliage: The bright green, long-stalked leaves are five-lobed with toothed margins. They are often attacked by the tar-spot fungus which causes large black patches to develop

Bark: Smooth, grey-brown, flaking into irregular plates

Flowers and fruit: The yellowish flowers grow in dense hanging racemes. The fruit, which are produced in pairs with wings held at right angles, spin like a helicopter's rotor blades when they fall thus aiding seed dispersal. They are green, tinged with varying amounts of red, but become brown with age.

General remarks: Also aptly referred to as Great Maple, due to its size, in North America this tree is known as the Sycamore Maple to distinguish it from a plane tree that is also called Sycamore. Its tolerance of polluted air has made it popular for planting in cities. The valuable white wood has little grain and it is used, among other things, for veneers, carving, furniture and making violins.

Acer pseudoplatanus

HOLLY

Ilex aquifolium

Family: Holly, Aquifoliaceae

Distribution: Indigenous to Britain, central, western and southern Europe and west Asia. It has been planted as an ornamental by gardeners across America

Crown: Young trees are conic, becoming irregular with age

Height: Up to 10 m (33 ft)

Foliage: The thick, shiny, oval leaves are dark green and leathery with sharp spines on their wavy margins. Leaves towards the top of the tree often have few or no spines. The foliage is often attacked by leaf-mining grubs which burrow between the upper and lower leaf surfaces

Bark: Smooth, pale grey

Flowers and fruit: The white, four-petalled male and female flowers are produced on different trees. The bright red berries which follow the female flowers are grouped in loose bunches

General remarks: Holly is commonly planted as a hedge. Many ornamental varieties have been cultivated by horticulturists including those with spineless or variegated leaves and yellow or orange berries. The hard, heavy white wood is utilized by cabinet makers and turners and is especially good for inlays and veneers. The berries are poisonous to man but are a favourite of Fieldfares and Redwings. The leaves and berries are used as one of the traditional Chrismas decorations. This species bears heavier crops of berries than its American counterpart.

Family: Olive, Oleaceae

Distribution: It is native to Eastern U.S.A. and southeastern Canada. Though brought to Britain many years ago it is rarely grown as it does not appear to be suited to the climate, its timber not being as good as that of the European ashs

Crown: High domed, conical or rounded

Height: Up to 24 m (80 ft), exceptionally to 30 m (100 ft)

Foliage: The leaves generally have from five to nine stalked leaflets that are a rich green above, silvery and sometimes hairy beneath. They may either have finely-toothed or smooth margins. In the autumn the leaves turn an attractive orange and purple

Bark: Dark grey with deep ridges

Flowers and fruit: It is dioecious with the male and female flowers produced in small purple clusters before the leaves unfold. The narrow brown seeds, or samaras, hang in bunches and are winged for only part of their length.

General remarks: Favouring moist upland soils it often grows in mixed hardwood forests up to 1,500 m (4,900 ft). It is America's most valuable native ash and its lumber is ideal for making a variety of sports equipment such as baseball bats, tennis rackets and polo mallets. Other uses include the manufacture of furniture, skis and snowshoes.

Fraxinus americana

COCKSPUR HAWTHORN

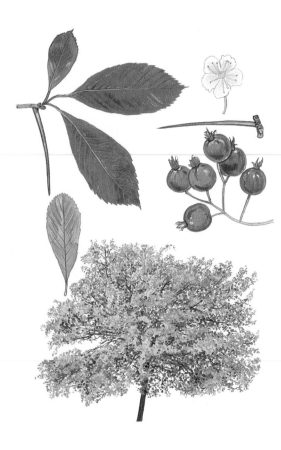

Family: Rose, Rosaceae
Distribution: Eastern U.S.A. and eastern Canada. Brought to Britain in 1691 and now quite common
Crown: Low and rounded
Height: To 7 m (23 ft)
Foliage: The oval dark green leaves have a finely toothed margin. In the autumn the leaves turn orange and red
Bark: Grey-brown, smooth with small cracks
Flowers and fruit: The five-petalled white flowers are borne in large clusters. The bright red berries contain two seeds.
General remarks: North American hawthorns, though they are a very distinctive group, are extremely difficult to distinguish from one another and only experts who have studied them can do so reliably. To further confuse matters they frequently hybridize with each other. This species, also called Hog Apple or Newcastle Thorn, grows as a shrub or as a small tree and its wood has the same uses as hawthorn. The branches are protected by very long, sharp thorns.

The berries often remain on the plant all winter thus providing a stockpile of food for wildlife at a time of scarcity. Sharp-tailed Grouse, Pheasants, Gray Fox and Whitetail Deer all utilize this resource. The flowers are important sources of honey and the dense foliage provides secure nest sites for many songbirds such as Brown Thrashers.

Crataegus crus-galli

Family: Rose, Rosaceae

Distribution: Native to Britain and across Europe to Afghanistan

Crown: Upright with a dense, rounded head

Height: Up to 10 m (33 ft)

Foliage: The small dark green leaves have three to five very deep-toothed lobes

Bark: Dark orange-brown, cracked

Flowers and fruit: The heavily scented, five-petalled white flowers grow in groups of 10–20. As they age the flowers become tinged to varying degrees with pink. The fruit is an oval crimson berry (haw) containing a large seed.

General remarks: White crab spiders frequent the flowers relying on their camouflage and stillness to catch their prey of flying insects. The appearance of the flowers in May gave rise to the colloquial name of May Tree. Hawthorn makes an excellent impenetrable hedge as the branches bear short, thick, strong thorns. Once widely grown in agricultural areas to mark field boundaries, modern farming practice has sadly encouraged the destruction of many miles of hawthorn hedge that used to provide a rich micro-habitat for wildlife. The hard wood is fine-grained and polishes well, but the small size of the timber limits its uses. It burns hot and slowly and also makes fine charcoal. The haws are eaten by Redwings and Bank Voles and the thick, thorny foliage provides birds with well protected nesting sites. Red-backed Shrikes store their excess insect or lizard prey by impaling them on the thorns.

Crataegus monogyna

ROWAN

Sorbus aucuparia

Family: Rose, Rosaceae

Distribution: Indigenous to Britain, it also is found in parts of Europe, North Africa and Asia Minor. It has been grown extensively in northern U.S.A. and Canada and is now established there in the wild

Crown: Irregular

Height: To 20 m (66 ft)

Foliage: The leaves are pinnate with five to seven pairs of green, serrated-edged leaflets

Bark: Silvery grey becoming grey-brown, shiny and smooth

Flowers and fruit: The flowers form dense, flat creamy-white inflorescences. The berries are green at first, turning yellow, then orange and finally scarlet.

General remarks: As its alternative name of Mountain Ash suggests, it can survive up to 2,000 m (6,560 ft). It grows higher than any other tree in Britain and prefers well-drained soils. The Latin name means 'a fowler', a reference to the fact that hunters used to prepare bird lime from its fruit which was smeared onto branches to ensnare small birds. The dense dark brown wood is used by turners and carvers and makes an excellent firewood. Mountain hares occasionally eat the bark in hard winters and the berries are much loved by Mistle Thrushes, Waxwings and Sable. Rowanberry jelly with venison is sav-oured by some, but to most its taste i rather harsh. The sweet-smelling flower attract a variety of insects that collect thei pollen and nectar.

Family: Legume, Leguminosae
Distribution: Scattered over mid-eastern U.S.A. Brought to Britain in 1812 but still rare
Crown: Broad rounded dome
Height: 15–20 m (50–66 ft)
Foliage: The drooping bright green shiny leaves are pinnate in form, with five to eleven alternate, large, elliptical leaflets. In the autumn the leaves turn a beautiful brilliant yellow. The brownish buds are quite hairy
Bark: Thin, smooth and dark grey or brown
Flowers and fruit: The small, white, pea-type flowers have five petals and are produced in a terminal panicle, a loose group of long-stalked flowers attached to a central stem. These fragrant flowers produce narrow pea-type pods containing 4–6 dark seeds. The pods drop off before they split open.
General remarks: One of America's most attractive flowering trees, it produces plentiful blooms only every two to five years. Some authorities give this species the Latin name *Cladrastis lutea*. It prefers rich moist soils, notably limestone. The heartwood, as the name suggests, is yellow though it does fade to pale brown on exposure to light. The wood was once used to make a yellow dye but otherwise has no great value.

Cladrastis kentukea

PACIFIC DOGWOOD

Family: Dogwood, Cornaceae
Distribution: Southern California northwards to British Columbia. Although brought to Britain in 1835 it is still uncommon
Crown: Dense, rounded or conical
Height: 10–15 m (33–50 ft)
Foliage: The large, oval, shiny green leaves are opposite and have a slightly wavy margin. Nearly hairless above they are covered with white woolly hairs below. The undersides turn brilliant red in the autumn
Bark: Thin, dark purple, smooth but becomes scaly
Flowers and fruit: The tiny green flowers are formed in tightly packed clusters at the centre of six large, cream white, occasionally pinkish, pointed bracts which are frequently confused with petals. The flowers and bracts develop in late summer, when they are purple and green, but only open in the following spring. The small orange or red fruits are borne in dense, globular bunches. They taste bitter and contain one or two seeds.
General remarks: As the Latin name suggests it is sometimes called Nuttall's Dogwood, after a 19th century botanist. Other names include Mountain and Flowering Dogwood, though the latter name is also used for an eastern species. They prefer moist mountainous soils up to 1,800 m (5,900 ft) and are often found in conifer forests. A popular ornamental, the tree presents a magnificent display when all the flower bracts, which cover the tree are open.

Cornus nuttallii

GLOSSARY

Anther: The part of the stamen containing the pollen sacs.

Aril: The exterior covering of the seed in certain plants.

Bole: The trunk of a tree from ground level to the first branch.

Boss: A knob-like protuberance.

Bract: A modified leaf at the base of a flower stalk.

Carr: A copse of alders.

Coppice: To cut down a tree leaving enough of the trunk to allow regrowth of branches.

Dioecious: Having the male and female flowers on separate plants.

Elliptical: Oval, but acute at each end.

Fastigiate: Erect, almost parallel growth, as certain branches.

Fissure: A narrow crack or split.

Glabrous: Smooth, hairless.

Globose: Round, shaped like a ball.

Hybridize: To produce a hybrid plant by fertilizing one species of plant with another.

Inflorescence: The arrangement of flowers in a flowerhead.

Lanceolate: Narrow, tapered at each end, like the head of a lance.

Lenticels: Small pores like corky spots on a young bark.

Ovate: Egg-shaped.

Panicle: A flower cluster, each of which has many stalked flowers, branching from a central stem.

Pedunculate oak: Having acorns on long peduncles on stalks.

Peduncle: A stalk or stem bearing a single flower or flower cluster.

Pinnate: With leaflets arranged on each side of a common stalk.

Plate: A thin, flat layer or scale.

Pollard: To cut back a tree to the main trunk to produce many new branches.

Raceme: An unbranched flower arrangement with individually stalked flowers.

Samara: Also called 'key fruit'. A winged, one-seeded fruit that does not split open to release its seed.

Serrated: Having the edge notched with toothlike projections.

Topiary: The clipping of shrubs into decorative shapes.

Variegated: Marked, spotted or decoratively patterned with a contrasting colour.